SUPER CITIES!

SAN FRANCISCO

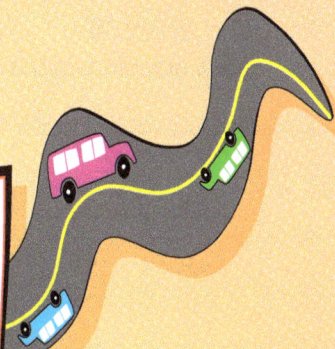

by James Buckley Jr.

arcadia®
CHILDREN'S BOOKS

Published by Arcadia Children's Books
A Division of Arcadia Publishing
Charleston, SC
www.arcadiapublishing.com

Super Cities is a trademark of Arcadia Publishing, Inc.

First published 2021

ISBN 978-1-5402-5066-7

Library of Congress Control Number: 2021943259

Notice: The information in this book is true and complete to the best of our knowledge. It is off ered without guarantee on the part of the author or Arcadia Publishing. The author and Arcadia Publishing disclaim all liability in connection with the use of this book.

Produced by Shoreline Publishing Group LLC
Santa Barbara, California
Designer: Patty Kelley

Contents

WELCOME TO

San Francisco!

FAST FACTS

San Francisco, California

POPULATION:
874,000

FOUNDED:
1776

NICKNAME:
The City by the Bay

San Francisco,
California

What do you call a city surrounded by water on three sides . . . often covered by fog . . . filled with steep, hard-to-climb hills . . . that has summers that feel like winters? Well, anyone who has been there calls it a little slice of heaven. San Francisco is one of the most famous cities in the world! Part of the reason is the huge Golden Gate Bridge, its most famous landmark. Since 1849, San Francisco has attracted people from around the world. It's a beautiful place filled with tons of things to do and see—and eat! Whether you ride a cable car, dig into sourdough bread, find a dragon in Chinatown, or walk across a famous bridge, San Francisco really has something for everyone. **California, here we come!**

SAN FRANCISCO: Map It!

San Francisco is on a peninsula, which means it is surrounded by water on three sides. To the west is the Pacific Ocean. To the north is the Golden Gate. To the east is the huge San Francisco Bay; across that water is the East Bay Area. San Francisco was built on very hilly land, so some parts of the city have amazing views across the Bay.

San Francisco, California

OREGON

NEVADA

Pacific Ocean

San Francisco

CALIFORNIA

Alcatraz
Island

Golden
Gate Bridge

Pier 39

Pacific
Ocean

North
Beach

Bay Bridge

Union
Square

San
Francisco
Bay

Market St.

Golden Gate Park

KEY

City limits

Parks

*San Francisco,
California*

Set the Scene

Here are some of the sorts of places you'll find on a visit to San Francisco.

The Bay: Stretching more than sixty miles from San Pablo in the north to San Jose in the south, the enormous San Francisco Bay is surrounded by more than a dozen small cities and towns. The city of San Francisco itself is on the west side of the Bay on a peninsula.

The Waterfront: Dozens of piers stretch out into the Bay. In the distant past, they were the landing places for thousands of ships of all sizes from around the world. Today, some still see fishing boats arrive with their catch. Others have become ferry landings for small boats that take people in all directions around the Bay. Some of the piers are now filled with shops, while others house museums.

Chinatown: While many cities have their own Chinatown, San Francisco's is one of the biggest and most famous. A part of the city since the late 1800s, Chinatown is a popular spot for visitors and locals alike to shop, eat, and stroll.

Market Street: Like a diagonal arrow through the middle of the city, Market Street is the "main drag" of the city. It stretches from the Ferry Building southwest to Hunters Point.

The Hills: The city was built on 43 hills. Steep streets go up and over them, making walking tough and driving an adventure!

SAN FRANCISCO MEANS . . .

Well, this one is easy. *San Francisco* is Spanish for Saint Francis. There are actually 88 people named St. Francis, but the one the city is named for was from Assisi, a city in Italy. In 1209, he founded an order of missionaries called the Franciscans. Franciscan priests were among the first white settlers to arrive in the Bay Area along with Spanish explorers in 1776. The Franciscans had been building churches called missions throughout California. Their leader, Fr. Junipero Serra, sent Fr. Francisco Palou to the Bay Area to build another one. It was named Mission San Francisco de Asis. It was also known as Mission Dolores, after a creek nearby that had been named for "our lady of sorrows" (*dolores* in Spanish).

However, the city itself was not named San Francisco at first. The city that grew around the mission building was called Yerba Buena, which means "good herb," or plant, in Spanish. San Francisco did not become the official city name until 1847.

Fr. Serra: Fr. Junipero Serra founded the first eight of 21 missions from San Diego to Sonoma. Their purpose was to convert the native peoples to Catholicism—by force if necessary. The local Native American peoples were forced to speak Spanish and farm and work for the community. The mission system had a strong impact on California, but leaves a terrible legacy.

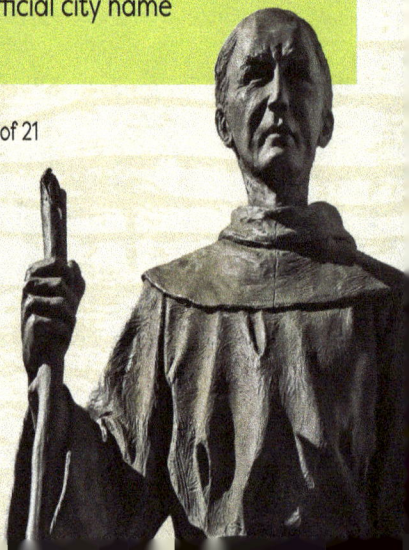

Mission Dolores

CABLE CARS!

In 1964, the cable cars were named an official National Landmark.

"The little cable cars climb halfway to the stars . . ."

That's what it says in the famous song, "I Left My Heart in San Francisco." Since they were first opened in 1873, people have been riding these rolling symbols of the city. The open-sided cars are pulled along by steel cables buried in the streets. Here are some key facts to know about these bell-clanging beauties.

Three cable car routes remain: Mason-Taylor; Powell-Hyde; and California.

At each end of their routes, the cars on the Powell and Mason lines have to be turned on a big roundtable. A platform rotates as the workers push the car around.

More than 10 million people ride the cars in a busy year.

The clanging bell is one of the most famous sounds in the city.

Each car weighs about 15,000 pounds and can fit 60 passengers (but sometimes more hang off the outside!). A one-way ride costs $7 and is worth every penny!

The cars are carried by steel cables that run beneath the street. A driver in each car operates a sort of claw that grabs the cable as it moves.

HISTORY: Early Days

People have lived on the San Francisco peninsula for more than 10,000 years. The Ohlone had villages and fishing spots there. They used boats to trade with other people that lived around the Bay.

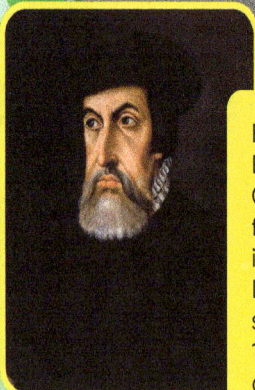

By the 1500s, explorers from Europe had reached the California coast. Hernán Cortes from Spain landed in California in 1535. England's Sir Francis Drake reached Port Reyes, south of San Francisco Bay in 1579. More Spanish people soon arrived, including the Franciscan missionaries in the 1700s.

1776: The same year that American colonists declared independence from Great Britain, the Franciscans founded their mission church in San Francisco.

1791: A larger mission building was dedicated. Restored over the years, it still stands as Mission Dolores in the heart of San Francisco.

Early 1800s: More and more Spanish settlers arrived in San Francisco, pushing the Ohlone farther and farther out. By the 1840s, perhaps only 1,000 Ohlone lived in the area.

1821: The lands of California (upper left in dark grey) were controlled by Mexico. In 1821, Mexico became independent from Spain.

The Bay provided fishing grounds for thousands of years.

1846: The Mexican-Amerian War started. The winner would control California, which was then part of Mexico. But some American settlers didn't wait for the war to end—they declared that California was free! The California flag that flies today was inspired by this group's "bear flag."

HISTORY: Early Days

1848: The Mexican-American War ended with America the winner. The lands that Mexico lost would become California, Arizona, New Mexico, and Texas—all now part of the United States.

John Sutter

1848: Life in San Francisco changed forever. About 130 miles to the east, on land owned by John Sutter, gold was discovered. Almost overnight, San Francisco bloomed from a small port to one of the busiest cities on the continent. Tens of thousands of people from around the world arrived by ship. They bought everything they needed to mine and then rushed to the gold fields. Some of them came back very soon. And very rich.

1849: San Francisco grew from about 1,000 people to more than 40,000. Along with people looking for gold, people came to make money from the prospectors ("prospectors" were the folks looking for gold). Stores opened, hotel rooms cost a lot, food was very expensive.

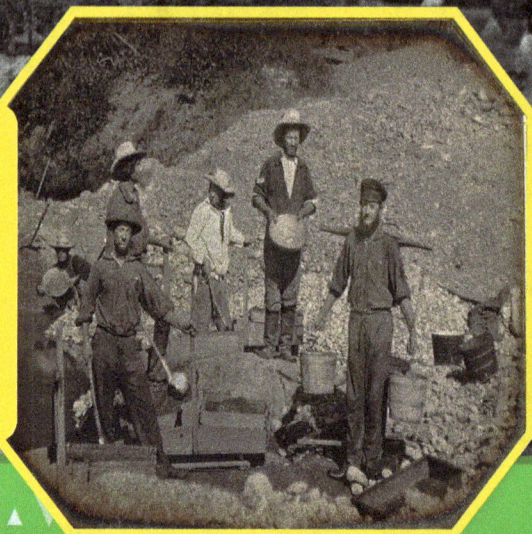

1850: The Gold Rush made California grow so much so fast that it became a state faster than any before or since. On September 30, 1850, it became the 31st star on the U.S. flag. The first capital city was San Jose, at the south end of San Francisco Bay.

1859: As if one "rush" was not enough, silver was found about 250 miles to the east. Another stampede of people poured into the city on their way to the silver mines.

San Francisco harbor scene, 1851.

HISTORY: Early Days

1860s: A group of businessmen from Sacramento banded together to create the Central Pacific Railroad to move people up and down the West Coast and to start to build toward the east.

1869: A transcontinental railroad track finally linked the East and West Coasts. The Central Pacific connected to the Union Pacific with the driving of the Golden Spike on May 12 in Utah. It meant that more people and goods could get to California faster than ever.

1873: As a way to conquer the city's many hills, the cable car system opened. In a few years, more than 600 cars were moving along 53 miles of cable car routes.

The Big Four

The four men who created the Central Pacific became enormously rich in the 1870s. Leland Stanford, Mark Hopkins, Charles Crocker, and Collis Huntington were known as the Big Four. (This picture includes Crocker's brother E.B. at upper left.) The Big Four's vast wealth built huge houses, hotels, ranches, libraries, and universities. They were called "robber barons" for their tough way of doing business. They helped build San Francisco, but they also demanded control and power.

The huge Mark Hopkins Hotel in San Francisco is named for one of the Big Four railroad "barons."

HISTORY: San Francisco Grows Up

1906: On April 18, a huge earthquake rattled the Bay Area. In seconds, dozens of buildings fell and thousands of others were damaged. Scientists have since figured out that the quake hit 8.4 on the Richter scale, making it one of the most powerful earthquakes ever recorded. Shortly after the quake stopped, a fire started among the wooden buildings of San Francisco. Over the next three days, 80 percent of the city burned up. Hundreds of thousands of people lost their homes and had to live in the streets.

1915: San Francisco showed off how far it had been rebuilt at a World's Fair that the city called the Panama-Pacific Exposition. Nearly 20 million people came to see huge exhibits, beautiful new buildings, and new inventions.

FAST FACT

The Palace of Fine Arts is the only building remaining from the 1915 Exposition.

1934: On an island in the Bay, Alcatraz opened as the most secure federal prison. For more on "The Rock," see page 42.

1936-1937: Just as the railroads connected east and west, two huge bridges connected San Francisco to other cities. In November 1936, the huge Bay Bridge opened to traffic. It went from San Francisco to the East Bay cities of Oakland, Berkeley, and others. Then the following May, the Golden Gate Bridge opened, connecting the city with Marin County and northern California. (See map on pages 6-7.)

Smoke from dozens of fires filled the air after the quake.

1941-45: The U.S. entered World War II in December 1941, after Japan bombed the U.S. at Pearl Harbor. In 1942, in response to anti-Japanese feelings, the U.S. government rounded up all people of Japanese descent (mainly on the West Coast) and sent them to camps in the California desert. With a large Japanese population, San Francisco was hit hard by this terrible and unjust practice. Tens of thousands of people—most of whom were American citizens—were forced to leave their homes and businesses. This is now recognized as one of the worst civil-rights violations in history.

MODERN TIMES

After the war ended, San Francisco became home to a lot of people looking to do things differently. Over the next 40 years, the city became a center for new ways of looking at life.

1950s: Poets and writers like Allen Ginsberg and Jack Kerouac created the free-spirited Beat movement. Reacting to the violence of the war, they looked for a new, peaceful way of life that focused on creativity.

Allen Ginsberg

1964: Across the Bay at the University of California at Berkeley, students began the Free Speech Movement (FSM). Inspired in part by the Civil Rights Movement in the South—which was calling for equal rights for Black Americans—the FSM called for everyone to be able to express their opinions, and for police and politicians to stop telling them what to do. It led to huge marches at UC Berkeley and in San Francisco.

Free Speech Movement leader Mario Savio at Berkeley.

1967: Young people were drawn to San Francisco by the Beats, the FSM, and a growing "hippie" movement. Huge concerts were held in Golden Gate Park (page 45) several times in 1967.

FAST FACT

In 2004, San Francisco became the first major city to make same-sex marriage legal. The law only lasted a month, but it was the start of a movement that has since seen marriage equality become approved in many states, including California, since 2013.

1970s: After the Beats of the '50s and student activists of the '60s, San Francisco's LGBTQ+ community grew and grew in the '70s. The city remains a national leader in fighting for equality for all people.

People from the Past!

Here are some San Franciscans who made a mark on history.

Levi Strauss (1829-1902)

Some of the Forty-Niners made their money in gold. Levi Strauss made his in denim. Born in Austria, he moved to San Francisco in 1853. He became very successful and in 1871 began selling denim jeans reinforced with metal rivets (which was a new idea!). Levi's are still popular around the world.

Emperor Norton (1818-1880)

Englishman Joshua Norton arrived in San Francisco from South Africa in 1853, hoping to make his fortune selling rice. Instead, he lost all his money. In 1859, he started a new career and became one of the wackiest characters in San Francisco history. He declared himself to be the Emperor of the United States! For the next 20 years, he entertained locals with proclamations about his wishes. He made up his own uniform and was seen regularly at bars and restaurants. He did have one good idea: He was among the first to suggest a bridge across the Bay to Oakland!

Lillie Coit (1843–1929)

In her youth, Lillie was obsessed with firefighters. As a teenager, she jumped in to help them pull hoses and ropes. She became like a mascot to several San Francisco fire companies. After she married a wealthy man, she donated lots of money to help the fire companies. After her death, she left enough money to build a huge tower in honor of the firefighters she loved. See page 40 for more on Coit Tower.

Isadora Duncan (1877–1927)

This San Francisco native was perhaps the most famous modern dancer in American history. In 1898, she moved from San Francisco to London, and she became an international star for her daring and beautiful dances, often barefoot, many inspired by classical statues.

The DiMaggio Brothers

One of baseball's most successful families came out of a fishing clan in San Francisco. All three DiMaggio brothers started playing for the hometown minor-league San Francisco Seals. Joe DiMaggio, the "Yankee Clipper," was one of the best players of all time. A three-time Most Valuable Player, he helped the New York Yankees win nine World Series in his career, which lasted from 1936 to 1951. Brother Dom was a seven-time All-Star star with the Boston Red Sox in 10 seasons. Vince DiMaggio rounded out the trio. When he made the 1943 All-Star Game with Pittsburgh, that made the DiMaggios the only trio of brothers to all earn that honor.

SAN FRANCISCO TODAY

The rich history of San Francisco all adds up to the great city it is today. It still has old-time style at the Wharf and other places. Its tall buildings show off its power as a business center. And millions of visitors make it one of America's top tourist spots.

Tech, Tech, Tech: San Francisco is home to dozens of technology companies (see page 62). They have brought in a lot of money to the city. Many tech workers live in the city, but commute south to Silicon Valley.

Tourism: Tens of thousands of San Francisco Bay Area workers make their money from visitors. Restaurants, tourist spots, ferries, shows, and more create a wide range of jobs.

Business and Finance: The city got rich with gold. So it makes sense that money is still a big part of San Francisco. Banks and stock-market companies fill the high rises in the busy downtown area.

LGBTQ+ Community: Starting in the 1960s, San Francisco became one of the most accepting places in the world for the gay and lesbian communities. They have found support in the city and have contributed enormously to the culture here. LGBTQ+ influence has spread and the city has been a leader in helping the fight for equal rights for all.

The Whole Bay Area

San Francisco is the main city in the Bay Area . . . but it's not the only one! To the south are small suburbs like San Mateo, Belmont, and Palo Alto. Marin County is to the north of the city. The northern waterway called San Pablo Bay is much less developed. Oakland is the biggest city on the East Bay, along with Berkeley and Fremont. At 1 million people, San Jose at the far south of the Bay is even larger than SF!

SAN FRANCISCO for Everyone

As the city's history shows, people have been coming to beautiful San Francisco from around the world for hundreds of years.

People from China

As a big city on the West Coast, San Francisco was the first place where people from China arrived by ship 175 years ago. The city became home to a large number of Chinese immigrants. They came to find work in building Western railroads and in the gold fields. Chinatown in San Francisco has been located near Broadway in North Beach since rebuilding after the 1906 earthquake. Things were very hard for Chinese San Franciscans who were treated badly and discriminated against as they worked to try to support their families.

By the 1960s, new laws made it easier for more people to move to the United States and the Chinese population grew again. Today, Chinatown is one of the city's most popular tourist destinations, and a favorite with locals looking to experience the culture, shop, and try out one of the many restaurants there.

Other Asia Pacific People

People from Japan, Korea, the Philippines, and other Asian countries also live and work in San Francisco, helping to make it one of the most diverse cities in the country. People from Korea and the Phillippines helped make places in their home countries into Sister Cities with San Francisco, too (see page 90).

Japantown is a vibrant part of the city focused on Japanese heritage, history, and culture. One part of that history is from World War II when the U.S. government forced Japanese Americans to sell their belongings and businesses and move into internment camps. When the war ended, they were released and worked hard to rebuild their community. Many years later, the government apologized for their terrible action and gave many of them money to repay some of what was lost.

Indigenous Culture

San Francisco became a focus of the struggle for Native American rights during the Alcatraz takeover in the early 1970s (page 42). A recent development hopes to build positivity. The city created the American Indian Cultural Center, which will include a place called "The Village" to provide resources for Native Americans as well as a way to educate people about the history, culture, and the impact of local tribes and the people who belong to them.

LGBTQ+ Life in the Bay Area

Since the years after World War II, San Francisco has become the most important city for the LGBTQ+ community. It has been the site of many important moments. The first Gay Pride Parade was held here in 1970; Pride Month remains a big annual celebration that has spread around the country. In 1972, Harvey Milk became the first openly gay person elected to a major city council; he became a leader in rights for LGBTQ+ people. The famous rainbow flag was designed here in 1978, and in 2004 the first legal same-sex marriage was peformed in San Francisco. As the city and its people showed a welcome spirit, more and more people in the LGBTQ+ community found a home here.

In the 1980s a new disease called AIDS hit the LGBTQ+ community in San Francisco badly. Thousands of people died in the city, and the national battle for support and treatment of the disease started here.

Today, the rainbow spirit is clear throughout the city. The Castro District was one of the first centers of LGBTQ+ life, and remains home to many bars, restaurants, and galleries, as well as a key location for Pride Month events. Few places are as accepting and welcoming to the LGBTQ+ community as San Francisco continues to be.

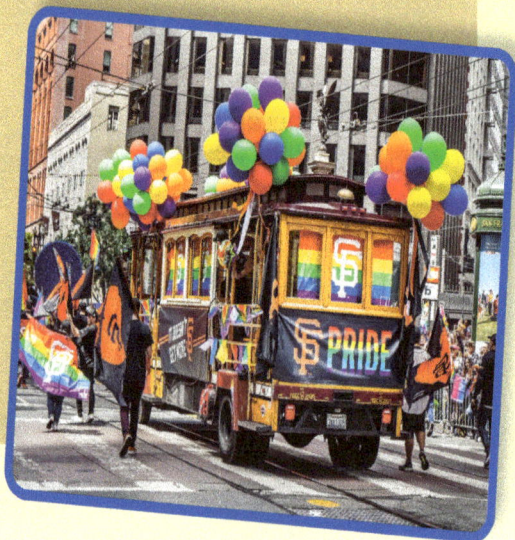

Black Life in SF

The African American population in San Francisco is small compared to other big cities. The Black community grew quickly during World War II, as many people came to work in the shipyards. But discrimination and segregation made it difficult for Black families in San Francisco.

Things were different, however, just across the Bay, in Oakland. After WWII, it became a national focus of Black culture. That city and others in the East Bay are filled with art galleries, restaurants, music sites, and museums that highlight the Black experience in the Bay Area.

FAST FACT
Willie Brown is a leading California politician who was mayor of San Francisco from 1996 through 2004.

Latinx People in San Francisco

People from Mexico and Central America have been part of the fabric of San Francisco from its very beginning. After all, California was part of Mexico for a time. A large number of people moved to the city and the Bay Area in the years after World War II, filling many jobs, including on nearby farms. Today, the neighborhood where many of those original immigrants lived, the Mission District, is a center for Latinx life in San Francisco. It's a great place to experience artistic, cultural, and celebratory events, as well as a wide variety of foods from many different Spanish-speaking countries.

Why Is It So Doggone Foggy?

San Francisco's Wacky Weather

Sunny California, right? Beaches, suntans, warm summer days! Well, if you expect to be warm in San Francisco all the time, think again. The famous writer Mark Twain once wrote that "the coldest winter I ever spent was a summer in San Francisco." He was being funny, of course, but San Francisco weather is most famous for being chilly when you don't expect it and foggy when it should be warm! So why all the fog? You can thank—or blame—science.

In the summer, hot air warmed by the sun meets the cold waters of the Pacific Ocean. When hot and cold meet like that, the air often turns to fog. The winds and breezes blow from the ocean toward the city and push the fog right in. You can sometimes see it rolling in clouds over the city's tall buildings.

Under that fog, a warm day can turn suddenly chilly. But just bring a couple of layers and you'll be fine. The fog makes for some beautiful and dramatic photos!

FAST FACT
San Franciscans try to take all the fog lightly. In fact, they give it a name: Karl the Fog.

This satellite view shows how the fog gathers over the ocean before rolling over the city.

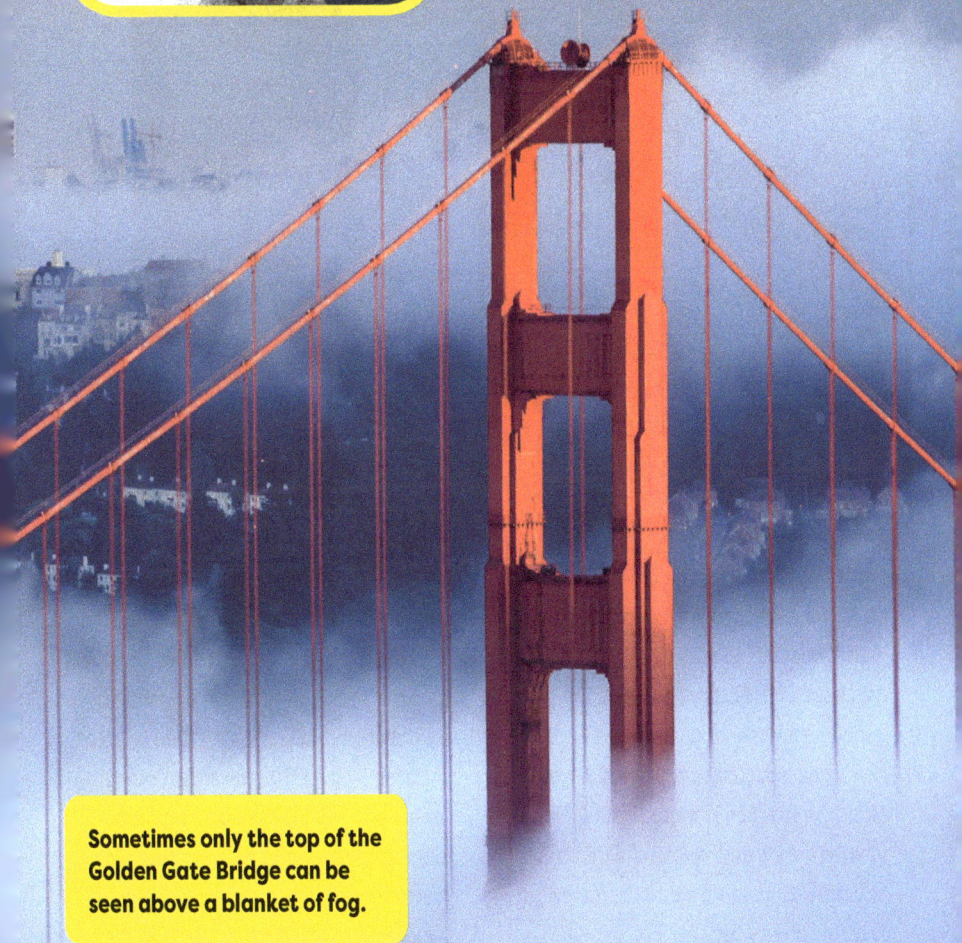

Sometimes only the top of the Golden Gate Bridge can be seen above a blanket of fog.

Hey! I Lived in San Francisco!

Thousands of amazing people have lived in the City by the Bay in the last 200 years (almost). San Francisco has especially inspired artists. Here's a quartet of memorable creative people.

Ansel Adams

Beatrice Wood

Ansel Adams was one of America's most famous photographers. He did almost all of his work in black-and-white. His pictures of western landscapes and of national parks are classics. He also photographed the Japanese relocation camps during World War II, and mountains and scenery in New Mexico. Born in San Francisco in 1902, he survived the big earthquake of 1906 with only a broken nose. He died in Monterey, just south of San Francisco, in 1984.

Beatrice Wood was born in San Francisco in 1893, but only lived there until she was six. Her family moved to New York City, and Wood later moved to France to be an actress and a painter. When she came back to the U.S. during World War I, she ended up in Los Angeles. By the 1930s, she chose pottery as her art form and moved to Ojai, near Santa Barbara. Over the next decades, she became one of the most famous artists in America. She lived to be 105 years old!

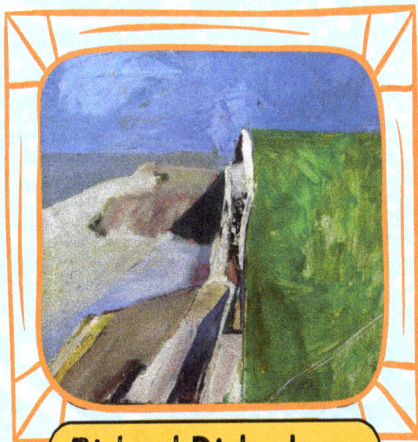

Richard Diebenkorn

Richard Diebenkorn was born in Portland, Oregon, but moved to San Francisco when he was two. He grew up there and attended Stanford and the San Francisco Art Institute (then called the California School of Fine Arts). His colorful, abstract paintings of ocean and city scenes helped make him one of the 20th century's most important American artists. He did most of his work in Santa Monica, but moved back to his Northern California roots late in life; he passed away in Berkeley in 1993.

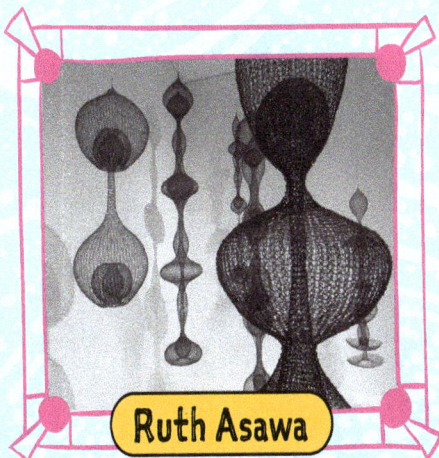

Ruth Asawa

Ruth Asawa was just 16 when she was forced, with her family, to move from her home in Santa Anita, California, into a relocation camp for Japanese citizens during World War II. After the war, she studied art and moved to San Francisco in 1949. She began a long and distinguished career as a sculptor, often using wire and metal to create amazing shapes and designs. She designed several large outdoor art pieces in San Francisco, including the fountain at Ghirardelli Square. She died in her SF home in 2013.

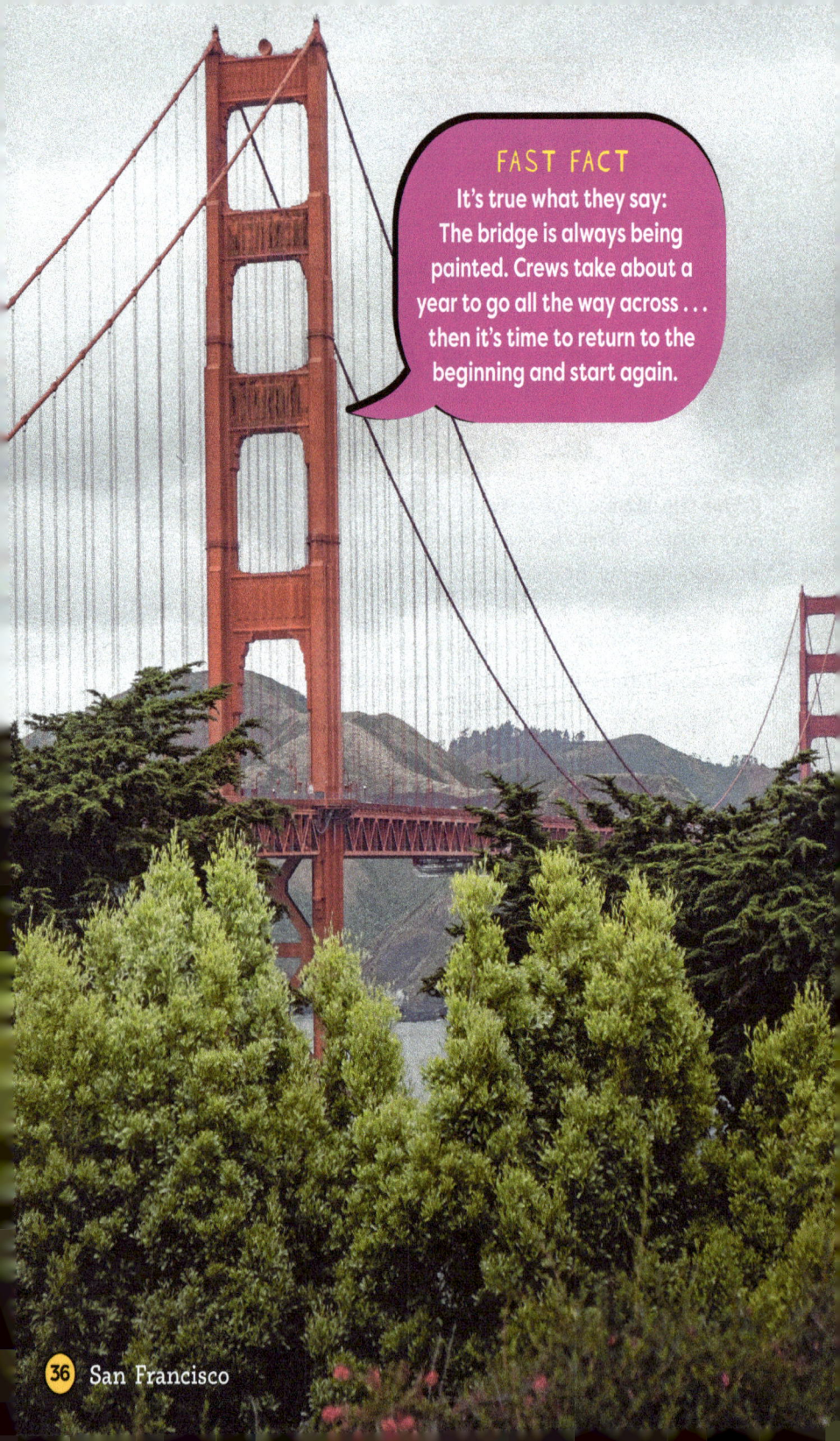

FAST FACT

It's true what they say:
The bridge is always being
painted. Crews take about a
year to go all the way across . . .
then it's time to return to the
beginning and start again.

Things to see in San Francisco

There is something interesting to see around just about every corner in San Francisco. Some of them are standouts, though, that you don't want to miss! This section gives you a sneak peek at the most famous spots.

Golden Gate Bridge

Trivia time: The name of this famous bridge actually came before the bridge! And it's not named for its color, either (which is officially called "international orange," not golden or red). Early explorers called the wide entrance to San Francisco Bay the Golden Gate. So when the bridge was built, choosing the name was easy. It opened in 1937 to cars and walkers. The bridge is 1.2 miles across the water, with another mile of roads leading up to it at each end. The top of the tallest tower is 746 feet above the water. Tens of millions of cars travel back and forth across the Golden Gate each year, while ships (and sometimes daring airplane pilots) whiz by underneath.

FAST FACT

Today's construction hard hats are modeled on headgear created for Golden Gate Bridge workers.

Fisherman's Wharf

SAN FRANCISCO'S TOURIST PLAYGROUND

At the northeast corner of the city, with great views of the Golden Gate and Bay bridges, Fisherman's Wharf is on every tourist's list of places to see in the City by the Bay. Here's a short tour, moving from west to east.

Ghirardelli Square: A huge chocolate-maker's headquarters stands over the western end of the Wharf area. Visit the store for dozens of kinds of sweet treats.

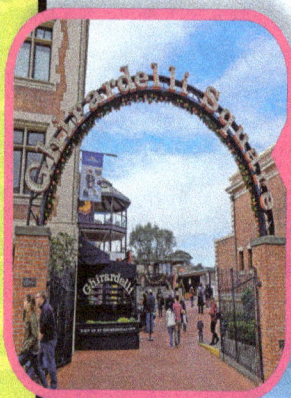

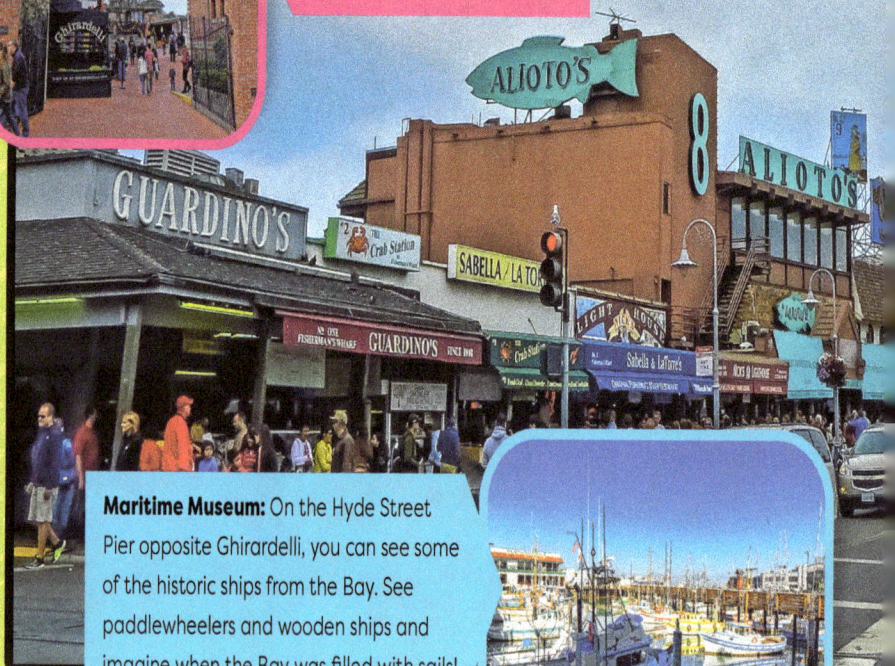

Maritime Museum: On the Hyde Street Pier opposite Ghirardelli, you can see some of the historic ships from the Bay. See paddlewheelers and wooden ships and imagine when the Bay was filled with sails!

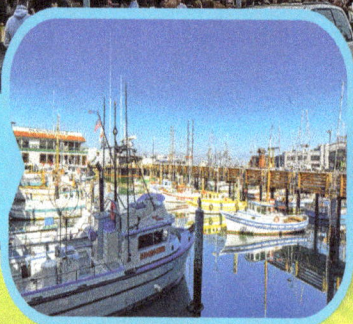

Ships of War: On Pier 45, take a trip to World War II by visiting the *Jeremiah O'Brien*, a Liberty ship, and the *Pampanito*, a submarine!

Museum Trio: The Ripley's Believe It or Not museum is filled with bizarre sights. The Wax Museum has statues of famous people made of (take one good guess). And the Musée Mécanique is a one-of-a-kind collection of antique arcade games—that you can play!

Pier 39: This entire wooden finger that sticks out into the Bay is filled with shops, restaurants, a carousel, and more. Here is where you can see the famous sea lions that have taken over piers where ships once floated.

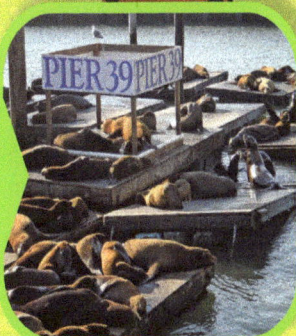

Bread!: Who doesn't like bread, right? The Boudin Bakery makes amazing sourdough bread (page 66) in crazy shapes. Watch in the window as bakers knead and form the dough, then go inside to try some!

San Francisco

The Ferry Building

Before cars and bridges, ferries took Bay Area people around their watery world. This building at the end of Market Street was where many of the ferries landed. Over the years, however, it mostly fell apart. In the 1990s, some very smart people helped restore the building and today it's a food-lover's paradise. Stroll under the historic arched ceiling and dig into food from around the world: candy, cheese, sandwiches, Asian delicacies, desserts, bread, produce, and much more.

Coit Tower

Standing 212 feet tall in Pioneer Park near Telegraph Hill, Coit Tower is one of the city's most famous landmarks. Built with money left by Lillie Coit (page 25), it gives visitors an amazing view of the Golden Gate and the Bay area. Murals in its base were painted in the 1930s and are also a great thing to see.

FAST FACT
Mythbusters! The design of Coit Tower is NOT based on the nozzle of a firehose! Myth busted!

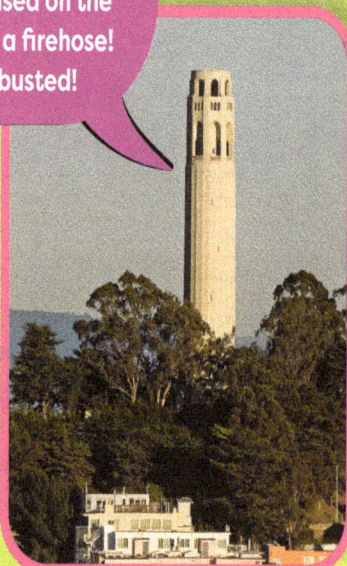

San Francisco is a city of neighborhoods. There are more than a dozen, and each has its own character and things to see. Here are three of the most famous and popular to visit.

Chinatown

Over the years, Chinatown has grown into a city highlight. Packed with antique shops, restaurants, tea houses, and gift shops, it's a one-of-a-kind adventure. A huge gate from Taiwan welcomes visitors, while beautiful temples and dragon statues give the area a unique feeling. Look for the fortune cookie factory, too!

Haight Asbury

At the eastern end of Golden Gate Park is a part of the city that became world famous in the 1960s. The neighborhood's apartment buildings, cafes, and clubs attracted young people. "The Haight" (HAYT) became a nickname for the entire hippie movement. It's still packed with tie-dyed clothing, thrift stores, and cool places to eat.

North Beach

This is San Francisco's "Little Italy," home to the best Italian food in the city. Established by Italian families who flocked to the area after the 1906 earthquake, North Beach today is home to a diverse group of young people and families.

Alcatraz

UNITED STATES PENITENTIARY

ALCATRAZ ISLAND   AREA 12 ACRES
1½ MILES TO TRANSPORT DOCK
ONLY GOVERNMENT BOATS PERMITTED
OTHERS MUST KEEP OFF 200 YARDS
NO ONE ALLOWED ASHORE
WITHOUT A PASS

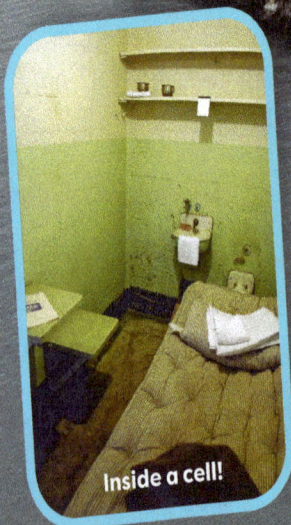

Inside a cell!

FAST FACT
The name comes from what Spanish explorers called the tiny island: *La isla de los alcatraces* (island of the pelicans).

This famous prison was a good argument for not getting into trouble! Alcatraz Island was first used as a fort, then a prison, by the U.S. Army in the 1800s. From 1934 to 1963, it was a maximum-security federal prison—the famous one you've heard about. Over the years, more than 1,500 criminals spent their days in cold, tiny cells as punishment for their crimes. Famous villains like Al Capone and "Machine Gun" Kelly were jailed there. It was famous for being tough, uncomfortable, and impossible (just about) to escape from. It was hard on guards, too, who had to live on the island with their families. Sometimes, inmates said they could hear the happy sounds of parties drifting across the water from the city. The prison closed in 1963 and became a National Park in 1972. Take a ferry to "the Rock" for a spooky tour of the cells and the forbidding grounds. Bonus: There are great views of the city skyline from Alcatraz!

Taking Over the Rock

In 1969, members of the American Indian Movement took over Alcatraz to protest the treatment of Native Americans. For more than 18 months, the group lived there to make their messages known.

Lombard Street

World's Twistiest Street

More than two million cars a year line up for blocks to make the slow, back-and-forth drive down this street in San Francisco. Tourists can also walk up (or down) a set of stairs alongside the street.

City Lights Bookstore

The famous Beat poet Lawrence Ferlinghetti opened this awesome shop in 1953. It is filled with books from around the world, and has a great children's section.

Golden Gate Park

Long, skinny Golden Gate Park slices through the western half of San Francisco. You can go for the museums (page 53), but there's lots to see and do without going into any buildings. The park includes a conservatory of flowers, an arboretum of trees, and several gardens with plants from around the world. Long meadows are great for walking. You can even spot a herd of American bison, not something you see everyday in the middle of a busy city!

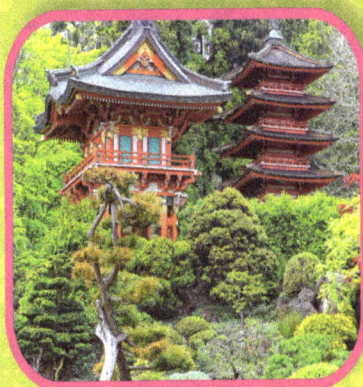

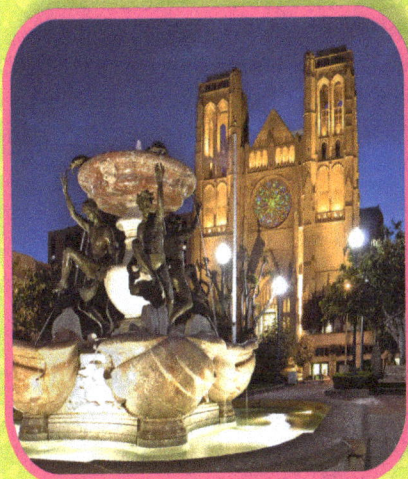

Grace Cathedral

Modeled after Notre Dame in Paris, this is one of the biggest and most beautiful churches in the city. On the floor of the main aisle is a labryinth. Walking its twisting path is supposed to help you think and meditate. You can also go to see the many stained glass windows— there are windows that honor Albert Einstein and John Glenn!

GETTING AROUND IN
SAN FRANCISCO

San Francisco is a hilly city, so walking a long way can be a challenge. There are still great hikes and paths to find, but when you need a quicker way around, here are some ways to go.

Subway: A network of underground trains links parts of the city with cities to the south and east. Bay Area Rapid Transit (BART) electric trains whoosh under the Bay through tunnels. They're a great way to beat traffic and see what lies beyond the city streets.

Streetcars: We already covered the cable cars (page 12), but the city also has a network of streetcars. These electric vehicles run on tracks, powered by overhead wires. The most famous ones run on Market Street. The cars are remodeled so you can imagine what it was like to speed along with people in the early 1900s.

Biking: With the arrival of e-bikes, moving through the hilly city by bike is much easier. Most major streets have bike lanes, and the parks also have long bike routes. The city is trying to expand the rental choices. But lots of bike shops are ready to rent visitors wheels.

Ferries: Two large fleets of ferries—the Blue and Gold and the Red and White—leave from the Ferry Building to places all around the Bay. Some people who work in the city actually take the boat every day like people in other cities use cars or buses. Taking a ferry is a fun ride, too, and a great way to see more of the Bay. Watch for dolphins!

IT'S OFFICIAL!

Cities like to name "official" things. That basically just means that lots of people who live there like something! Here are some of San Francisco's "official" city things.

OFFICIAL TREE:
Uncle John's Monterey Pine, in GG Park

OFFICIAL CITY SONG:
"I Left My Heart in San Francisco"

"I Left My Heart in San Francisco" is the most famous song about the city. But a song named for the city from a 1936 movie of the same name is the second "official" song.

OFFICIAL CITY INSTRUMENT:
Accordion

OFFICIAL CITY FLOWER:
Dahlia

OFFICIAL CITY BIRD:
California quail (oddly, there are none still living in SF!)

SAN FRANCISCO

OFFICIAL CITY MOTTO:
Oro en Paz, Fierro en Guerra
(gold in peace, iron in war)

Bay Bridge Lights: The flashing, brilliant displays of light can be seen around the Bay at night.

Wood Line: Following one of the Presidio's many winding paths, this creation by artist Andy Goldsworthy is huge, more than 1,200 feet long!

Art in San Francisco

Art is everywhere in San Francisco, inside museums and on the streets where you walk. One of the most visible displays of outdoor art is the Bay Bridge itself. In 2013, artist Leo Villareal put more than 25,000 LEDs on 1.8 miles of the towers and wires of the bridge. The flashing, colorful, energetic display lit up the night. It was supposed to stay up for only a short time, but became so popular that it was made permanent in 2016. Here's a look at some other cool outdoor art; turn the page for more ways to experience SF art.

Outdoor Art

People in San Francisco love being outdoors. Artists have created lots of fun things for visitors and locals to check out.

Language of Birds: Do books fly? They do in Chinatown, where this overhead sculpture hovers above the street. Check it out at night when it lights up!

Vaillancourt Fountain: Some people love this huge collection of metal forms with flowing water, built in 1971. But some people hate it! Check it out near Market Street and the Embarcadero.

Skygate: This twisty metal sculpture was put up in 1985, kicking off a new growth spurt of outdoor art.

Art Museums

SF Museum of Modern Art:
Known as SFMoma, this art-filled building opened in 1995. It specializes in art of the past century, but really shines when featuring artists from the Bay Area itself. And there are lots!

Cartoon Art Museum
This museum celebrates cartoons, comic strips, comic books, anime, and graphic novels, and the folks who bring them to life.

DeYoung Museum: See art from Asia, Africa, and Oceania in this cool building in Golden Gate Park. But that's not all: The DeYoung also has lots of American art, by famous artists including Georgia O'Keeffe and Ruth Asawa. And visit the huge observation deck to see just how big Golden Gate Park really is!

Museum of Craft and Design: Not all art is made with paint and marble. This museum celebrates the many ways that people have used traditional methods to bring beauty to everyday life.

Asian Art Museum: Paintings, sculpture, textiles, and objects from many centuries fill this old building near City Hall. The collection includes work from China, Japan, Korea, and other Asian countries.

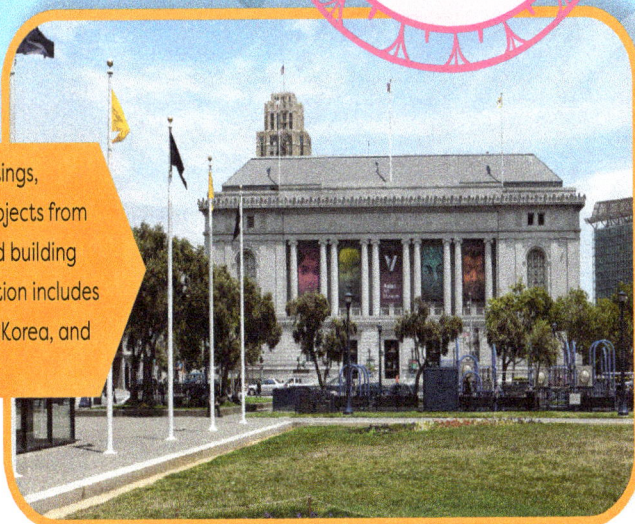

Other Great San Francisco Museums

Museums are great for more than just art, of course. San Francisco has some awesome museums to explore.

Exploratorium: On Pier 15 at Fisherman's Wharf, this science-focused museum lets you touch just about everything. You don't just look at exhibits, you take part in them—measure, experiment, build, create, design, and more.

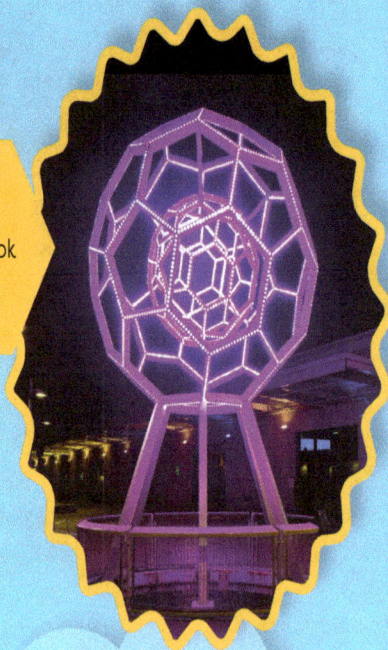

California Academy of Sciences: What do you call a place where you can go under the sea, into the stars, and around the world . . . and see grass growing on its roof? In Golden Gate Park since 2016, the California Academy lets visitors see plants, animals, and more, while also showing off its own unique building (the "living roof" helps keep the building cool!).

Legion of Honor Palace of Fine Arts: This is the only building left over from the 1915 Pan-Pacific Exposition. And it was built by sugar! Alma Spreckels inherited her family's sugar fortune. She used it to help pay for this art museum, which was modeled after a famous building in Paris, France. Check it out in the park near the west end of Fisherman's Wharf.

Museum of African Diaspora: MoAD is an art museum that celebrates Black cultures and inspires learning about the global impact of the African Diaspora (which consists of the millions of people around the world who descend from African men and women taken from their native lands, mostly during the slave trade).

Performing Arts

While rock music (58-59) is one of San Francisco's most famous arts, the city is also filled with people sharing their incredible talents. Performing artists from around the world head to the Bay Area to play at some of these places.

San Francisco Opera House
Opened in 1932, this classic building is home to the San Francisco Opera Company and San Francisco Ballet.

SF Jazz Center:
This center for jazz music opened in 2013. It has a large auditorium for big shows, and a smaller space for jam sessions and small concerts.

Louise Davies Symphony Hall
The San Francisco Symphony is the main performer here, but concerts by artists of all kinds are held year-round.

Theaters
San Franciscans love to go to the theater. Plays and musicals fill stages big and small all over the city.

They Made the Music

For more than a century, San Franciscans have created some of the most important and memorable music in U.S. history. Jazz was born in New Orleans in the 1920s, but San Francisco had its own version by the 1930s. After World War II, big-band jazz was loved by millions, but rock music was coming by the 1950s.

It was the 1960s that really put San Francisco on the musical map. In those years, the city attracted a ton of new acts who helped change rock-n-roll. Guitarist Jimi Hendrix, singer Janis Joplin, the groups Grateful Dead and Jefferson Airplane, and many others made San Francisco THE place to see the greatest new acts in rock.

Some of the new music was inspired by folk music. The social protests of the 1960s also inspired musicians. A highlight came in 1967 during the "Summer of Love." Huge concerts in the city's parks brought young people from around the world. They danced, sang, hung out, and then carried their love of the new music back home.

In the 1970s, Carlos Santana brought Latin flavor to rock music. Creedence Clearwater Revival mixed country, folk, and rock for a softer sound. In the 1980s, punk rock arose led by the Dead Kennedys and Faith No More, among others. In the 1990s and early 2000s, Bay Area fans joined the rise of hip-hop, watching local heroes like E-40.

Rock, pop, and hip-hop are still heard at dozens of live-music clubs in the Bay Area.

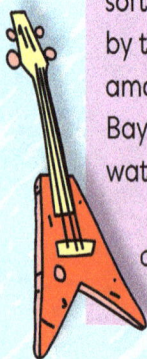

Some Famous Musicians with SF Roots

Counting Crows
Dead Kennedys
Grateful Dead
Green Day
Jefferson Airplane
Jimi Hendrix
Janis Joplin
Journey
Metallica
Steve Miller Band
Linda Ronstadt

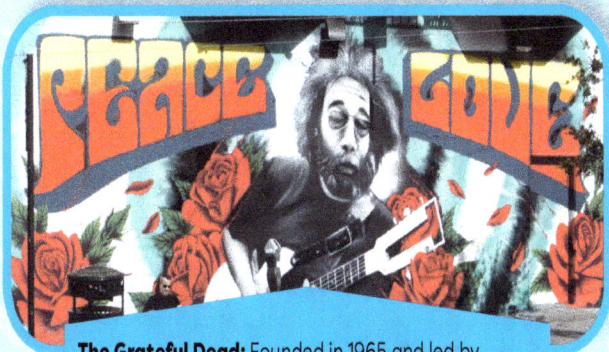

The Grateful Dead: Founded in 1965 and led by guitarist Jerry Garcia, this group was probably the most famous to come out of the city in the 1960s. They combined rock, folk, bluegrass, and lots of tie-dyed clothes. Though many original members have since died, some continue to play concerts to devoted fans.

Sly and the Family Stone: Other than Jimi Hendrix, few Black artists were part of the San Francisco rock scene in the 1960s. An exception was this popular group led by Sly Stone. The group combined rock with rhythm-and-blues and soul music. The "family" was diverse and included female members, too.

Green Day: This group from the East Bay was part of the punk-rock movement, but soon grew beyond those roots. Their fast-paced music and sometimes wacky lyrics have made them enormously popular starting in the 1990s, and earned them twenty Grammy Award nominations. One of their albums, American Idiot, was made into a Broadway musical!

How to Talk San Francisco

Just about every place in the world has some words that only make sense to locals. Here are a few examples of "only in San Francisco" words or phrases.

THE CITY

People in San Francisco are pretty sure they live in the best place in the world. So they just say "the city," instead of the city name. And when you're heading back to San Francisco, just say you're "going to the city" and everyone will know what that means.

THE TOWN

This is what San Franciscans call Oakland, their neighbor across the Bay.

415

Like many places, people in San Francisco use their area code as shorthand.

Hella

An adjective that means really great. "This sourdough bread is hella good!"

Yee

This one is a bit older, so you might not hear it often, but longtime SFers use it instead of "yes."

SAN FRANCISCO: It's Weird!

Like all cities, San Francisco has quirky traditions. But we've just picked a few examples to feature!

Dress to Run!

What do you call a running/walking race combined with Halloween? It's the Bay to Breakers! A run across the city that started in 1906, it has become a day-long party. Many of the runners wear costumes as they jog or walk the 7.5 miles. Crowds line the route to cheer for their favorite outfits. Some people dress together, so you might see a 12-person centipede or a train or even a bridge jogging along!

FAST FACTS
The 1986 Bay to Breakers run included a Guinness World Record 110,000 runners!

Karl the Fog

San Franciscans are stuck with fog (page 32). So instead of just hating it, they learn to live with it. To make it easier, they gave it a name. Karl the Fog even had a kids' book written about him! Say hi next time you're in the foggy Bay!

Parrots of Telegraph Hill

In the middle of the big city is a forested hill with steep wooden steps. They wind up through small houses. And living in the trees are . . . parrots! The first of these colorful birds (likely escaped pets) showed up in the 1990s. The flock has grown to hundreds. Visitors and locals enjoy seeing the flashes of green and red zipping above the steps.

Yabba-Dabba-House

It's a bit south of the city, but this one-of-a-kind house is worth the trip. You can see it as you drive on highway 280 near Hillsborough. And yes—it looks like the Flintstones cartoon! The family home includes several colorful, round cement buildings like some sort of real-life cartoon. It's been turning heads since it was built in 1976.

San Francisco

What People Do

IN SAN FRANCISCO

More than 875,000 people live in San Francisco itself. But that jumps to nearly eight million people if you include nearby cities and towns around San Francisco Bay. Here are some of the most popular ways that people make a living in this area.

Technology: Silicon Valley, to the south of the city, is home to dozens of the biggest tech companies in the world. Some of them have their headquarters in San Francisco itself, including Salesforce, Uber, Airbnb, Twitter, Yelp, and Lyft. Tens of thousands of people work in programming, marketing, and sales.

The Arts: music, art, culture, drama, dance, and much more are a big part of San Francisco. Thousands of people work hard to entertain and create for audiences who come from around the world.

money: In the years after the Great Fire of 1906, San Francisco grew rapidly. That took money, so banks grew quickly here. Wells Fargo, Bank of America, and VISA all still have their HQs here. San Francisco is also one of the biggest West Coast cities for financial companies working in the stock market.

millions of people come to San Francisco to have fun . . . and tens of thousands of local folks work to make that happen. Hotels, restaurants, tour guides, and attractions employ folks of all ages all around the area.

Clothing: Levi Strauss (page 24) remains a big employer in San Francisco, more than 100 years after it was founded. The GAP and Old Navy are two other huge clothing companies based here.

Hey! I'm from the Bay Area . . .

Kamala Harris
Born in Oakland: 1964
In 2021, Harris became the first female Vice President of the United States and the first person of color to hold the office. She is a former U.S. Senator for California, and got her start in the Bay Area as the San Francisco District Attorney.

Steve Jobs
Born in San Francisco: 1955
Jobs teamed with Steve Wozniak to found Apple Computers in 1976. Over the next three decades (until his death in 2011) Jobs helped create some of the most famous computer products ever—the Mac, the iPhone, and the iPad. He also helped start the animation studio Pixar.

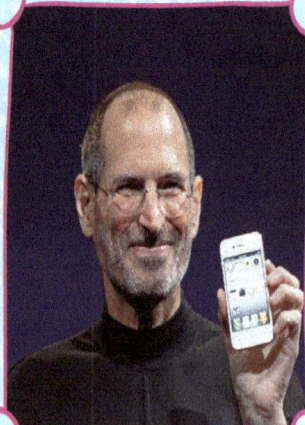

Harvey Milk
Came to SF: 1972

In 1977, the former Navy officer and businessman became the first openly gay city council member in San Francisco. His leadership paved the way for helping the whole LGBTQ+ community gain new status and rights in San Francisco, California, and the world. Sadly, his work and life were cut short when he was shot by a fellow politician in 1978. He remains a hero to all who fight for civil rights.

"NYIRAMACHABELLI"

DIAN FOSSEY

1932 – 1985

NO ONE LOVED GORILLAS MORE

REST IN PEACE, DEAR FRIEND

ETERNALLY PROTECTED

IN THIS SACRED GROUND

FOR YOU ARE HOME

WHERE YOU BELONG

Dian Fossey
Born in San Francisco: 1932

Fossey's love of animals and conservation made her a world hero, especially for her work with mountain gorillas in Rwanda. She spent so much time with them, they became like family. Her work helped create safe places for the gorillas to live and inspired animal lovers worldwide. She died in 1985.

Eat the San Francisco Way

If you love seafood, you'll LOVE San Francisco. Fresh food from the water can be found in lots of restaurants and stores—from salmon and seabass to crabs, clams, and oysters. But that's not the only type of food that people in San Francisco enjoy.

Clam Chowder Few things are more "San Francisco" than diving into clam chowder that fills a carved-out loaf of sourdough. Visitors to Fisherman's Wharf get to eat the tasty local version of the famous chowder . . . and then eat the bowl!

Chocolate Domingo Ghiradelli opened his first chocolate shop in San Francisco in 1849! By 1893, his shop and factory were on the square near Fisherman's Wharf. The famous giant sign was first lit in 1923.

GHIRARDELLI

A type of bacteria helps give sourdough its unique taste. When it was discovered, it earned a name in honor of the bread's famous home: *Lactobacillus sanfrancisensis.*

Sourdough Bread

San Francisco bakers did not invent this bread—but they did make it perfect. When hungry gold miners arrived in the 1850s, they found that sourdough bread baked perfectly in the Bay Area. Some said it was the foggy air. Some said it was the local water. Some said it was the local bacteria. However it happened, sourdough has been linked to SF ever since. A famous bakery at Fisherman's Wharf draws big crowds, but the bread is sold all over.

The It's It

Since 1928, this famous ice cream sandwich has been a San Francisco treat. George Whitney combined two oatmeal cookies, a blob of ice cream, and chocolate coating. They are still made in the Bay Area. Dig in!

Italian Food

Some of the first immigrants to San Francisco came from Italy during the Gold Rush. They brought their many styles of food with them. By the early 1900s, the North Beach neighborhood was packed with Italian restaurants. It's still a great place to find all sorts of pasta, sauces, olive oil, and Italian specialties.

Go, San Francisco Sports!

San Francisco is home to some awesome pro sports teams. Go, team, go!

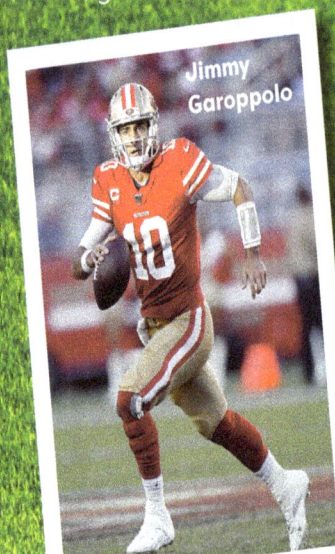

Jimmy Garoppolo

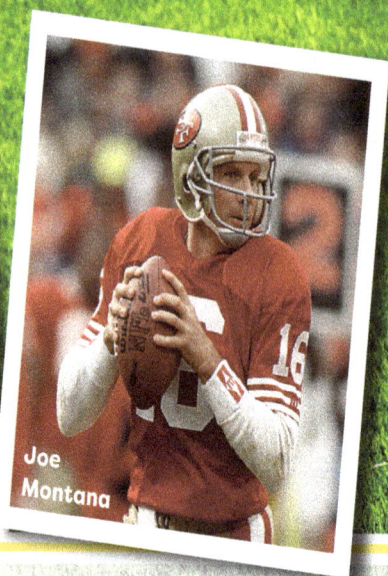

Joe Montana

SAN FRANCISCO 49ERS

Joined the National Football League in 1950 after four seasons in the All-America Football Conference.

The Niners once played in Golden Gate Park and later at Candlestick Park in south San Francisco. They last reached the Super Bowl in the 2019 season.

Cool Stuff: The Niners won four Super Bowls in the 1980s.

Big Names: Joe Montana, Jerry Rice, Steve Young, coach Bill Walsh

Home: Levi's Stadium (in Santa Clara)

SAN FRANCISCO GIANTS

Joined Major League Baseball in 1883*.
*The team was the New York Gothams for two years, and then became the New York Giants until 1957. Then they moved to San Francisco, where they now play at a ballpark on the waterfront.

Cool Stuff: McCovey Cove, where home runs land in the water; the giant baseball glove in the left field stands; winning three World Series from 2010 to 2016.

Big Names (SF years only)**:** Willie Mays, Willie McCovey, Will Clark, Buster Posey, Madison Bumgarner

Home: Oracle Park

Buster Posey

OAKLAND ATHLETICS

Joined Major League Baseball in 1901*.
*The Philadelphia Athletics started in 1901, the first year of the American League. The team moved to Kansas City from 1956 to 1967. Since 1968, they have played in Oakland.

Cool Stuff: Won three World Series in a row from 1972 to 1974; they also won in 1989.

Big Names (in Oakland)**:** Reggie Jackson, Vida Blue, Jose Canseco, Rickey Henderson

Home: Oakland Coliseum

Stephen Curry

GOLDEN STATE WARRIORS

Joined the NBA in 1949.

*The Philadelphia Warriors were part of the first NBA season in 1949, after three years in the old Basketball Association of America. The team moved and became the San Francisco Warriors in 1962. They took their current name in 1971.

Cool Stuff: Led by the Splash Brothers—Stephen Curry and Klay Thompson—the Warriors won three NBA titles from 2015 to 2018. The Warriors played in San Francisco until 1971, when they moved to Oakland. In 2020, they moved back to San Francisco into a new arena.

Big Names: Wilt Chamberlain, Chris Mullin, Rick Barry, Stephen Curry

Home: Chase Center

SAN JOSE EARTHQUAKES

Joined Major League Soccer in 1996.

Cool Stuff: The Quakes were one of the first teams in a new league. The team was first known as the Clash, switching to its current name in 2000. They the MLS Cup in 2001 and 2003.

Future U.S. national-team star Landon Donovan was the MLS MVP when San Jose won it all in 2001. Chris Wondolowski is the MLS all-time goals leader!

Big Names: Donovan, Wondolowski, Dwayne DeRosario, Jeff Agoos

Home: PayPal Park

SAN JOSE SHARKS

Joined the National Hockey League in 1991.

The Sharks brought pro hockey back to the Bay Area. The California Golden Seals had moved to Cleveland in 1976.

Cool Stuff: The Sharks' best season came in 2015-16 when they reached the Stanley Cup Final.

Big Names: Joe Thornton, Patrick Marleau, Brent Burns,

Home: SAP Center

COLLEGE TOWN

Few American regions are home to as many top colleges and universities as the San Francisco Bay Area. Tens of thousands of students from around the world study here every year.

UNIVERSITY OF CALIFORNIA, SAN FRANCISCO

Founded 1864
Students: 3,300
Popular majors: medicine, nursing, dentistry
Fast Fact: UCSF only has graduate students, all working in health and medicine.

UNIVERSITY OF CALIFORNIA, BERKELEY

Founded 1868
Students: 32,000
Popular majors: Engineering, biomedicine, computer science
Fast Fact: This school is called simply "Cal" by students and alumni, and is often ranked among the top public universities in the world.

STANFORD UNIVERSITY

Founded 1885
Students: 7,000
Popular majors: Engineering, computer science, social sciences
Fast Fact: Full name is Leland Stanford Junior University, but the "Junior" is for the son of the railroad baron. Stanford students helped create Google and lots of other Internet startups.

SAN FRANCISCO STATE UNIVERSITY

Founded 1899

Students: 26,000

Popular majors: Business, communication, social sciences

Fast Fact: This is part of a 23-school Cal State system. The school mascot is an alligator, or Gator for short . . . and a pun on Golden *Gater*, get it?

SAN JOSE STATE UNIVERSITY

Founded 1857

Students: 28,000

Popular majors: Marketing, business, health/medicine, visual arts

Fast Fact: This is the oldest public college on the West Coast!

SANTA CLARA UNIVERSITY

Founded 1851

Students: 5,500

Popular majors: business, social sciences, engineering

Fast Fact: Santa Clara is run by the Jesuits, an order of Catholic priests.

CALIFORNIA COLLEGE OF THE ARTS

Founded 1907

Students: 1,500

Popular majors: architecture, animation, graphic design

Fast Fact: Originally including "and Crafts" in its name, the school was in Oakland and San Francisco until moving to a new campus in San Francisco, south of Market Street, in 2022.

California College of the Arts

LOL!
San Francisco Sillies

Go ahead and laugh at San Francisco—its people won't mind! Here are some riddles to tickle your funny bone.

Why is the Golden Gate Bridge orange?

It was painted that color!

How did San Francisco's Ocean Beach get its name?

Nobody is shore.

What do cows make after a San Francisco earthquake?

Milk shakes!

Where do letters grow in San Francisco?

In the Japanese Tea Garden.

What's the difference between a satellite dish and cable?

San Francisco doesn't have satellite dish cars.

What do you get when two 49ers walk into a restaurant?

Ninety Aters

Why does the United States mint in San Francisco make special coins, but not regular coins?

I don't know – it doesn't make cents!

It's Alive! Animals in San Francisco

San Francisco is a pretty busy city of buildings and streets and people. But there is still lots of room for animal life of all kinds!

Invaders!

In about 1990, large packs of sea lions started hopping out of the Bay and onto the wooden platforms of Pier 39 (see page 39, really). Pretty soon, there was no room for boats or people. The sea lions became a popular attraction. People lined the walkways to watch the big sea mammals loll around and bellow!

Birdland

What do you get when you have a lot of water? A lot of water birds. Marshes, beaches, and rivers all around the Bay Area attract millions of birds. Pelicans, ducks, geese, and gulls are common. The forests that remain to the north of the Bay are also home to many songbirds like the red-winged blackbird.

Jaws! The cold waters of the Pacific Ocean off of San Francisco are home to one of the fiercest predators around—the great white shark! The deadly creatures are often seen by fisherfolks leaving from the Bay. The Farallon Islands to the west of downtown are a famous shark-sighting spot. Sadly, some swimmers and surfers have been bitten near northern California beaches.

San Francisco garter snake

The city gave its name to this colorful local reptile. There used to be many more of these animals, but all the housing ruined many of their habitats. Still, they are almost as colorful as the city they are named for!

Don't Touch! This little critter is so cute and colorful, you want to pick it up! Don't! The California newt has poison on its skin. They live in wooded areas along the coast.

WE SAW IT AT THE ZOO

Animals have been on exhibit in San Francisco since at least 1866. In the late 1890s, a famous grizzly bear named Monarch attracted big crowds to his home in Golden Gate Park. The San Francisco Zoo that visitors enjoy today began in 1929. It is in the southwest corner of the city. More than 2,000 animals roam the grounds in dozens of awesome exhibits.

Gorillas

Bears

Penguins

Lemurs

Giant cockroaches

Oakland Zoo

Across the Bay is another great place to see animals. The Oakland Zoo, which opened in 1922, also has an African Savanna exhibit. You can also see flamingos, big cats, lots of animals native to California, and some from Australia. The children's part of the zoo is perfect for hands-on fun while you help feed the critters.

One Big Park!

The Presidio

The northwest corner of the city of San Francisco is where it all began. Spanish explorers built their first fort there; *presidio* means "fort" in Spanish. It was later where Mexican troops were stationed until 1848, when it was taken over by American forces. The huge area includes Fort Point, former army barracks, and memorials. In 1994, the U.S. Army turned the entire area over to the National Park Service. The Presidio has become San Francisco's playground, with hiking and biking trails, picnic areas with amazing Golden Gate views, and historic sites and museums to explore.

Walt Disney Family Museum

In buildings where soldiers once slept, ate, and played, this colorful museum has been open since 2009. Exhibits, videos, and galleries tell the life story of Walt Disney, the man behind so many movies and, of course, Disneyland and Disney World.

Spooky Sights

Do you believe in ghosts and spirits? Not everyone does . . . but no one knows for sure! Like most cities, San Francisco has lots of places that people say are haunted.

Alcatraz Few places in the world are said to be as haunted as the Rock. The prisoners who died there have left an eerie, chilling feeling to the place. Visitors have been creeped out by voices and footsteps. Some cells make people feel the presence of long-dead inmates. Cell 14D is supposed to be especially haunted. And before it was a federal prison, Alcatraz held Native Americans captured by the U.S. Army. The prisoners' clanking chains have been heard in the clammy cement hallways.

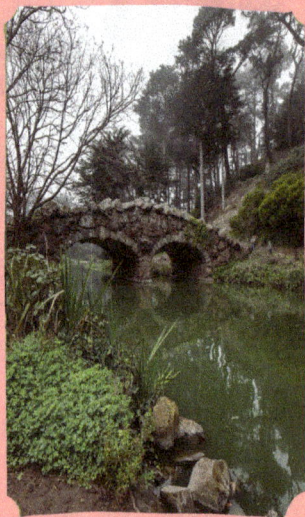

Golden Gate Park: A legend that is more than a century old tells of the "White Lady" who haunts Stow Lake. The story goes that she lost her baby in an accident and has been searching for her ever since.

Cliff House: This huge wooden building used to stand on the Pacific shore. Legend says that a ghost named Natalia haunts the grounds, as she waits and waits for her beloved to return from World War I.

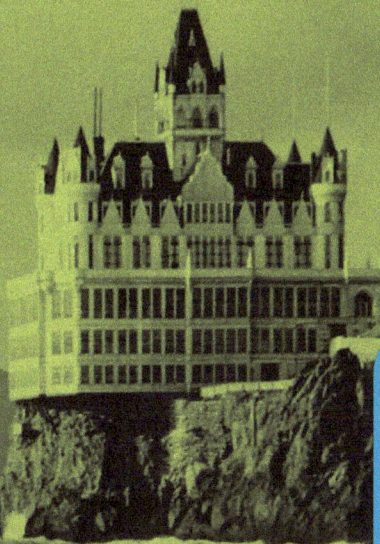

Sutro Baths: Near the Cliff House, these saltwater pools used to attract thousands of bathers in the early 1900s. They eventually fell out of favor and were finally knocked down in 1966. Since then, visitors say they've seen ghostly people walking around the grounds, perhaps waiting their turn to swim!

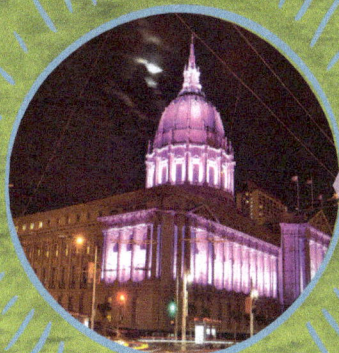

City Hall: What do you get when you build on top of a cemetery? Ghosts, of course! Yerba Buena's oldest cemetery became the land for City Hall, where spirits and ghosts have been seen for more than 100 years.

Not Far Away

Whether you live in San Francisco or you're just visiting, don't forget that many other awesome places to visit are very close by. Get a driver and hit the road for these fun day (or so!) trips.

How about this view? We took a trip up to Marin County.

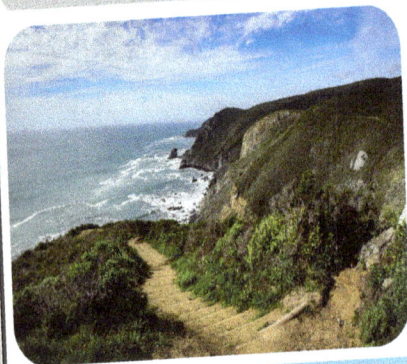

Wow! Where did you take that pic?

That's the Marin Headlands. It's part of the Golden Gate Recreation Area just on the other side of the big orange bridge!

😲 Jealous!

There are hiking trails and places to bike and there's even a small redwood forest to explore.

Where else did you go?

My parents loved the vineyards.

In Marin and other places to the north, people grow lots of grapes for wine.

And grape juice!

Totally! It's beautiful farm country.

Don't look down when you're in a car here!

Beautiful! ¿Donde?

We drove south from SF to Big Sur. Incredible views of the ocean.

Glad your dad was driving!

Yeah, I spent the whole ride glued to the window. We also camped here.

Awesome! Take me next time!

While we were down there, we went to the Monterey Bay Aquarium. This giant tank is packed with fish!

Hope you didn't go fishing! 😃

Ha! No, just watching. The otters were super-cute.

Not Far Away

Oaktown! That's what people call Oakland.

East Bay Rules!

Yup! We took a drive across the Bay Bridge to explore Oakland and that area.

Fave place?

You'd think it was cheesy, but Fairyland was fun! It inspired Walt Disney way back when. The Oakland Zoo rocks, too.

Let's go!

We also visited Berkeley, home of the Univ. of Calif. We ate at this famous hot dog place.

Order one for me!

The campus is beautiful and there's a nice botanic garden.

Go Bears!

Keep studying. Maybe we can go there together!

Remember the Gold Rush?

Not personally, but I did read about it! 😊

Ha! Well, we took a drive to see where it started.

On the river?

We drove on a road. But they found gold in a river three hours east of SF.

While we were there, we went to Sacramento. It's been the capital of California since 1855.

Why not San Francisco?

Gold rules! And that's where the gold was!

Sister Cities Around the World

Did you know cities can have sisters? Why not brothers? Well, that's just what they're called. Sister Cities was started in 1956 as a program of the U.S. government. The idea was to connect cities here and around the world to help people get to know each other. This was not long after World War II, so making new friends was pretty important! San Francisco jumped on board quickly and today is a Sister City with 20 places around the world!

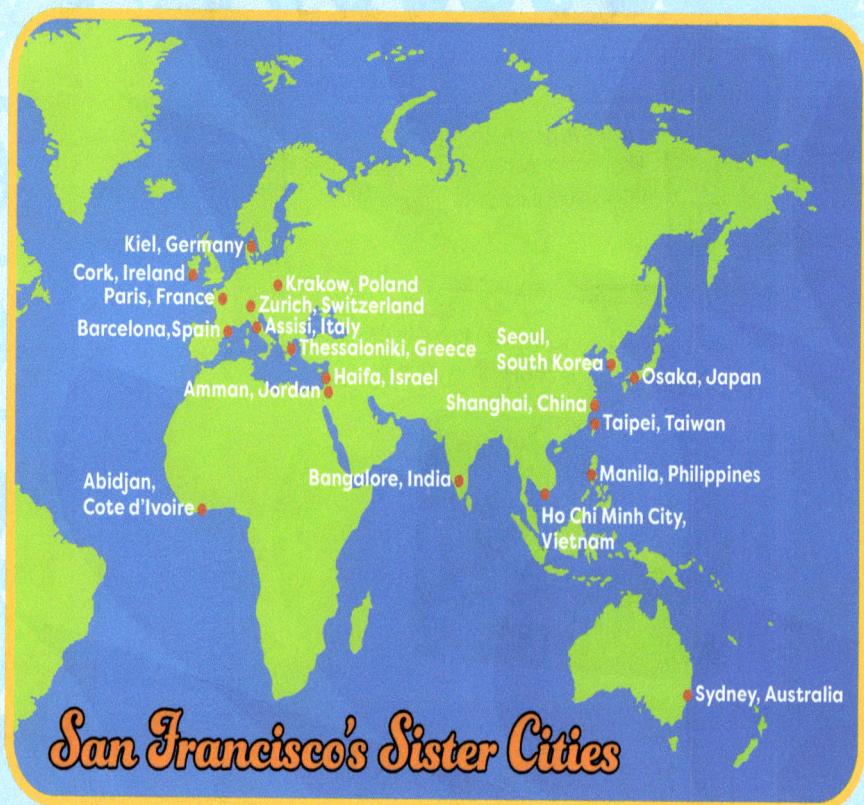

Kiel, Germany
Cork, Ireland
Paris, France
Barcelona, Spain
Krakow, Poland
Zurich, Switzerland
Assisi, Italy
Thessaloniki, Greece
Amman, Jordan
Haifa, Israel
Seoul, South Korea
Osaka, Japan
Shanghai, China
Taipei, Taiwan
Abidjan, Cote d'Ivoire
Bangalore, India
Manila, Philippines
Ho Chi Minh City, Vietnam
Sydney, Australia

San Francisco's Sister Cities

Sister Cities in Action

Here are some examples of how San Francisco is working with and helping its sister cities:

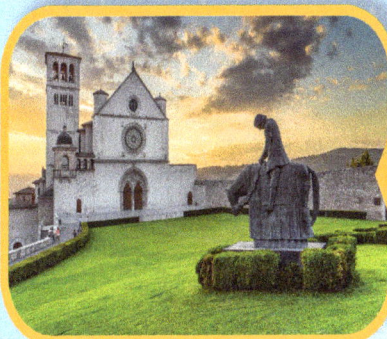

Seoul: Both sister cities have a version of this bronze sculpture, known as the Korean Monument. It was designed by Man Li Choi in honor of the first visit to SF by Koreans in 1883.

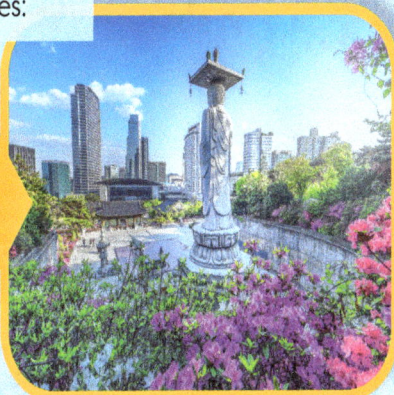

Taipei: The gate at the entrance of Chinatown is a gift from Taipei, Taiwan, to its sister city. There is also a building at Stow Lake in Golden Gate Park that honors the friendship.

Haifa: The two cities didn't let a pandemic stop them. In 2021, the Haifa Museum of Art teamed with SF's Contemporary Jewish Museum for an online art exhibit featuring creations by artists in the two cities.

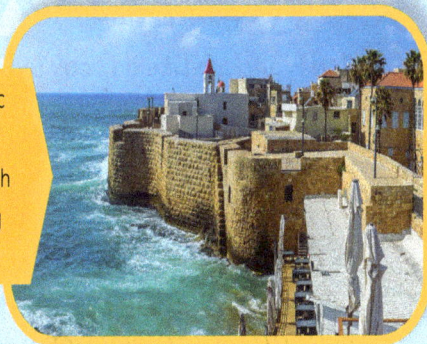

Assisi: San Francisco is no stranger to earthquakes. So when a bad quake rocked Assisi in 1997, San Franciscans raised money to help rebuild the Italian town.

Books, Websites, and More!

Books

Coleman, Ted. *San Francisco 49ers All-Time Greats.* North Star Editions, 2021

Ogintz, Eileen. *Kid's Guide to San Francisco.* Globe Pequot, 2014.

Rygh, Charlotte. *Shrimp 'n Lobster: A San Francisco Adventure.* The Collective, 2021

Sasek, Miroslav. *This Is San Francisco.* Originally published 1962; republished by Universe, 2003.

San Francisco Like a Local: By the People Who Call It Home. DK Eyewitness, 2021

Web Sites

hhttps://www.bayareakidfun.com/
Things to do and see, plus camps, activities, and more.

https://sf.curbed.com/maps/things-to-do-sf-kids-places
Show this site to parents to help find fun things for your whole family in the City by the Bay.

https://bayareadiscoverymuseum.org/
Located in Sausalito, on the north end of the Bay, this fun site has activities for fun, learning, and creativity for all ages.

https://www.exploratorium.edu/
No visit to SF is complete without time spent playing (and learning) at this Pier 15 experience.

https://www.sftourismtips.com/san-francisco-with-kids.html
A tourism site offers lists of fun things to do with kids!

www.sftravel.com
A one-stop shopping spot to find out tons of info about visiting San Francisco.

Photo Credits and Thanks

Photos from Dreamstime, Shutterstock, or Wikimedia unless otherwise noted.

Flickr: Coetzee 51; Ruth Hartnup, 54B. Focus on Sports: 62L, 63BR. National Archives: 20C. Newscom: Gary Bogdon/KRT 57; Nick Wosika/Icon Sportswire 64L. NOAA: 30B. Seattle Municipal Archives: 14C, 16T, 16L, 16C, 18C, 63T. Visit Seattle: 10, 14L, 34C, 38, 39B, 47B, 48-49-50 (all), 66B, 67B, 77R, 78.

Artwork: Shutterstock: Spreadthesign 8L; LemonadePixel 24B, 31TB, 42B, 58-59; danceyourlife 43B, 51. Maps (6-7): Jessica Nevins.

Cultural Content Consultant: Jennifer E. Ellwood.

Thanks to our pal Nancy Ellwood and the fine folks at Arcadia!

INDEX

Thanks for Visiting
SAN FRANCISCO
Come Back Soon!